T0158232

CREATED BY

EDVARD

&

· ·

Look! It's Edvard Munch, working in his studio.

Can you guess what his job is?

Edvard likes to work in many different ways. He paints, he draws, he prints.

He works on paintings that are small and some that are ginormous.

He paints pictures that are sad and angry but also many that are happy and harmonious.

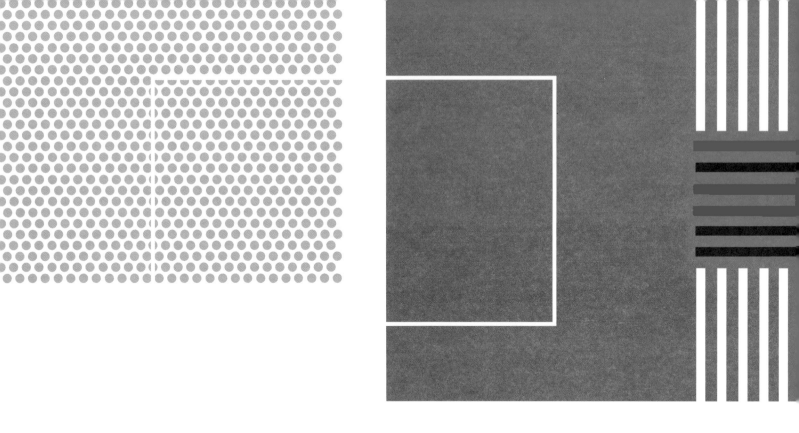

Edvard likes to look at everything that surrounds him.
He sketches people, trees, animals, houses and more.
He likes to experiment and play!
Why don't we join him and make art inspired by his?
Pencils ready? Let's have fun just like Munch!

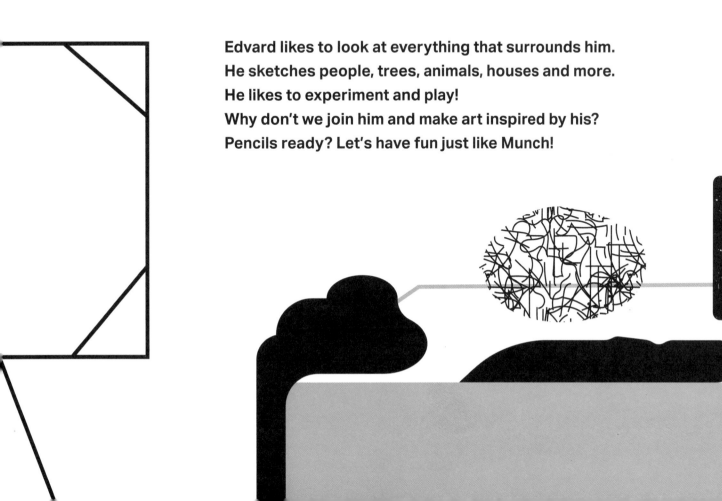

Do you recognise this building?
This cool new museum in Oslo is home to a massive collection of Edvard's art.
If you go inside you will notice the use of many different materials
and heaps of space. Can you complete the lines on the outside?

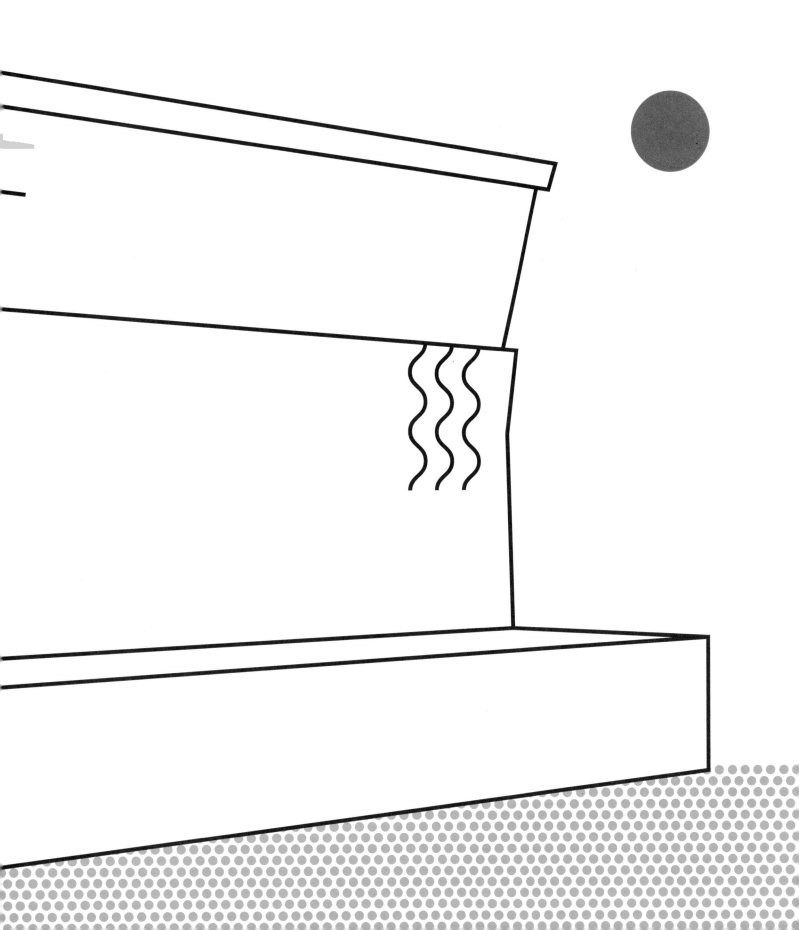

How would you design your own museum?
Would it look like something out of this world?
Draw your project below.

If you look at Edvard's paintings you will notice trees painted as different shapes.
What kind of tree shapes can you draw? You can use the stencil if that helps!

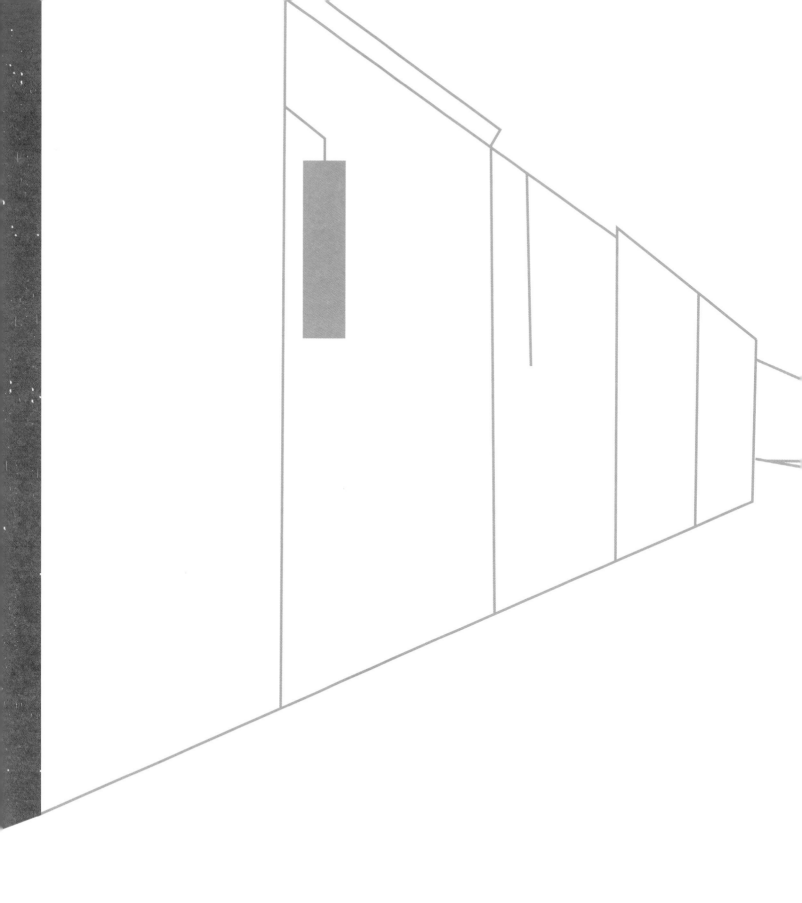

The street Karl Johans gate is usually full of people.
Fill it with your own interesting characters.

A motif you might recognise from many of Munch's paintings is a moon
and its reflection in the water. It looks like the letter 'i' as well.
What else could you turn the shape into?

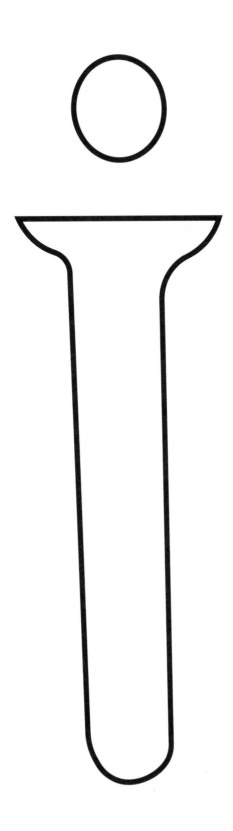

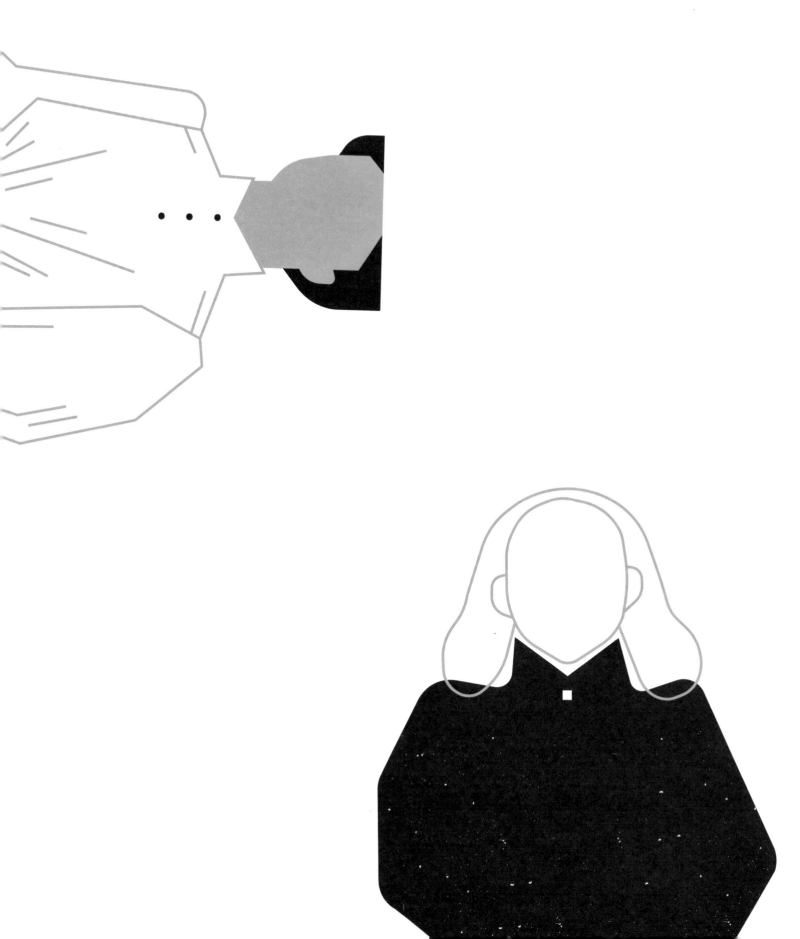

Many artists, including Edvard, drew and painted things they saw around them.

Can you find five objects and draw them?

Make sure you keep looking!

One of Edvard's paintings is called *The Wedding of the Bohemian*.
But look, the guests have nothing to eat!
Can you fill the table with food they can enjoy?

Fill this page with happy scribbles.

Fill this page with angry scribbles.
Which colours can you use?

Evening. Melancholy is a painting which portrays the character feeling sad.
Can you change the meaning of it by filling it with happy and colourful things?

Did you know that Edvard often painted animals?

Add your favourite animals next to the ones you see on this page.

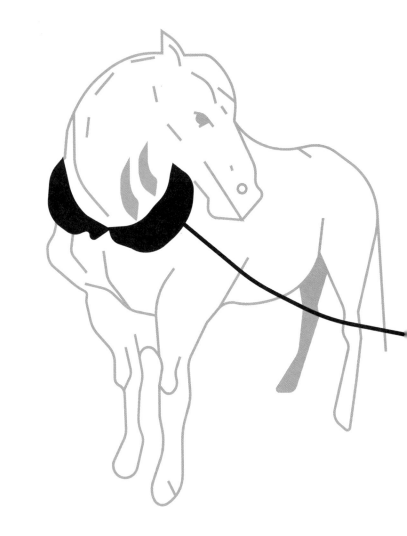

Fill this apple tree with as many green apples as you can.
What could you draw next to it?

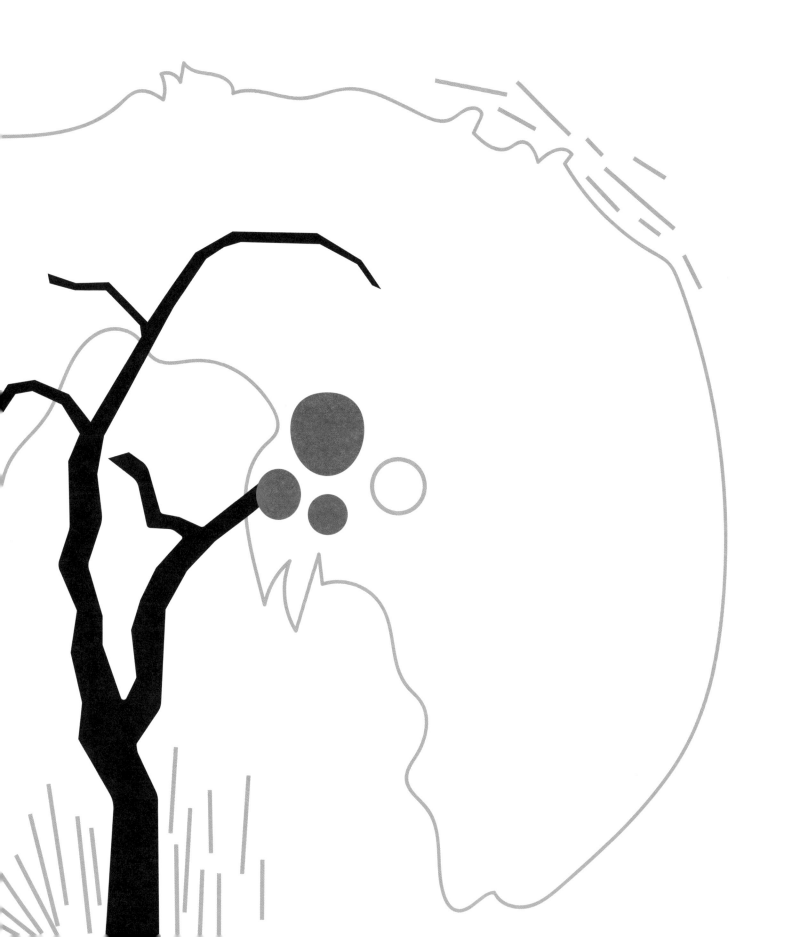

These people look very plain. Can you make their clothes fun?

Edvard often painted self-portraits and even took 'selfies' with his camera.
Can you draw a self-portrait next to his?

Here is a shape from a famous painting by Edvard.

Can you guess which one and change the shape into something different?

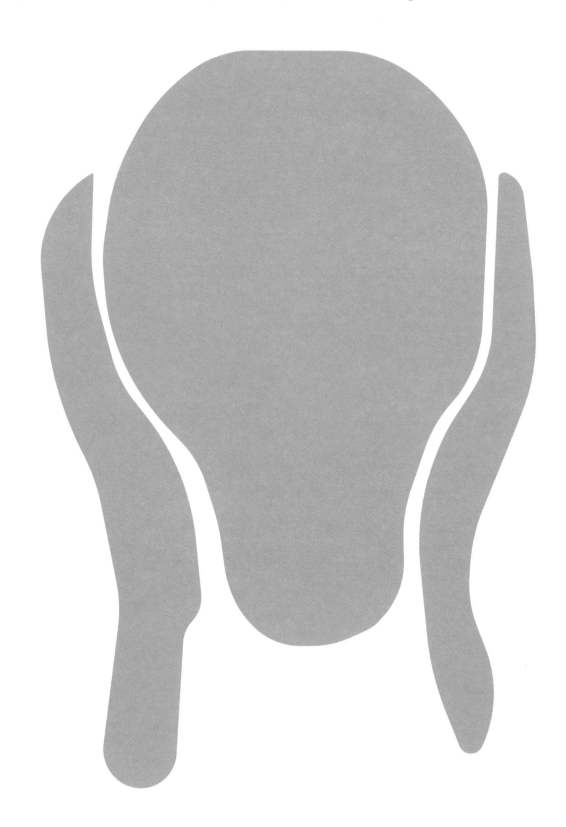

Now trace the shape from the stencil a few times.
What could they become?

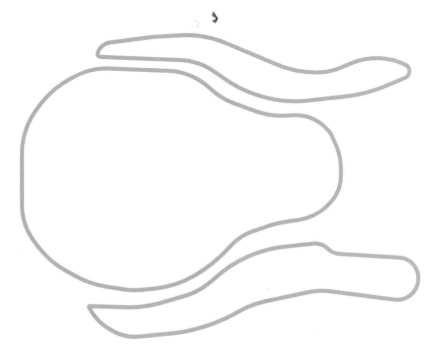

Edvard didn't finish his painting called *The Island.*
Help him by filling the sea with different shades of blue.

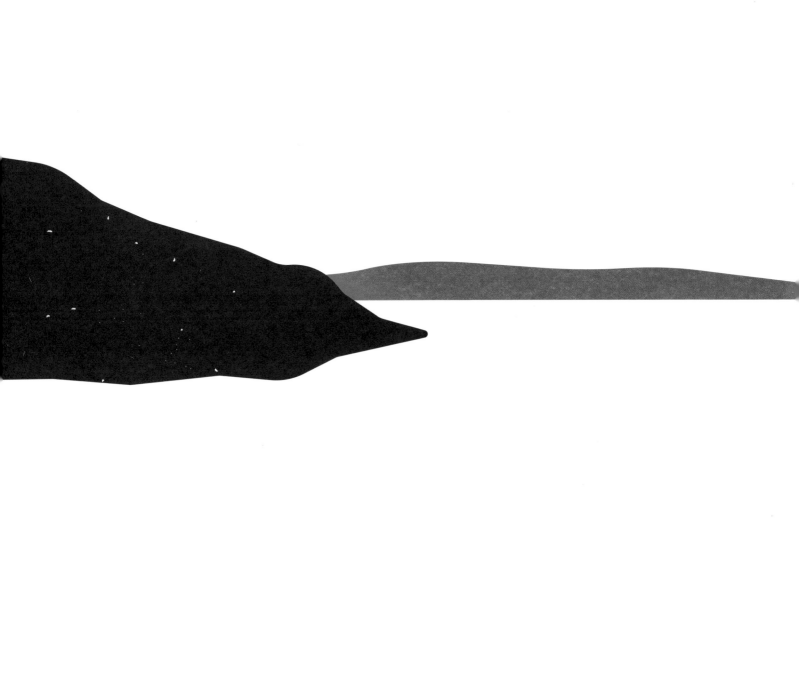

Draw your favourite dream.

In the painting *Red Virginia Creeper* you see this house.

Draw houses you see in your neighbourhood.

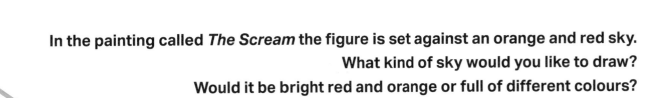

In the painting called *The Scream* the figure is set against an orange and red sky.
What kind of sky would you like to draw?
Would it be bright red and orange or full of different colours?

Design eye-catching shirts using stencils.

Who lives in this house?

Can you draw what's inside?

Design fun pattern using three colours.

Look, Edvard didn't finish his painting called *Melancholy*.
Help him by drawing the view from the window.

Draw what the girl could be thinking.

Create the biggest and most colourful sun you can!

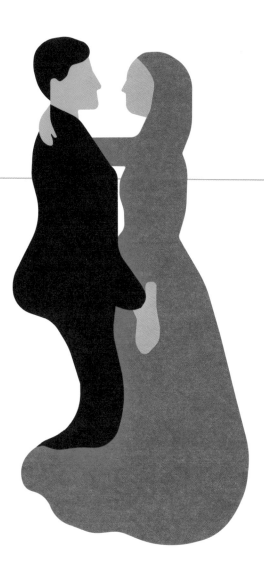

This party looks very dull.
Fill the pages with dancers and party fun!

Look at the pictures and find six differences.

Ekely is a place where Edvard lived and worked surrounded by beautiful nature.

Can you use colour to bring his garden to life?

Did you know that Munch loved surrounding himself with his paintings?
He often painted motifs he liked again and again and used them for inspiration.
Can you fill his studio with your creations?